Turbulent Planet

Storm Warning
Tornadoes

EXPRESS EDITION

Chris Oxlade

Raintree

Chicago, Illinois
VERNON AREA PUBLIC LIBRARY DISTRICT
LINCOLNSHIRE, ILLINOIS 60069

For information, address the publisher:
Raintree, 100 N. LaSalle, Suite 1200, Chicago, IL 60602

Printed and bound in China
Color Reproduction by Dot Gradations Ltd, UK
10 09 08 07 06
10 9 8 7 6 5 4 3 2 1

Library of Congress Cataloging-in-Publication Data

Oxlade, Chris.
    Storm warning : tornadoes / Chris Oxlade.
        p. cm. -- (Turbulent planet)
    Includes bibliographical references and index.
    ISBN 1-4109-1740-1 (library binding-hardcover) --
    ISBN 1-4109-1750-9 (pbk.)   1. Tornadoes--Juvenile literature.
    I. Title. II. Series.
    QC955.2.O952 2005
    551.55'3--dc22
                                    2005005691

This leveled text is a version of Freestyle: Turbulent Planet: Storm
Warning.

Acknowledgments
p. 4/5, Frank Lane Picture Agency/David Hoadley; p. 5 top,
Corbis Sygma; p. 5 middle, Frank Lane Picture Agency/ David
Hoadley; p. 5 bottom, Frank Lane Picture Agency/H. Hoflinger; p.
6, Corbis/Marc Rebutini; p. 7 Frank Lane Picture Agency/David A.
Robinson; p. 8/9, Science Photo Library/Jim Reed; p. 8, Science
Photo Library/Howard Bluestein; p. 9, Science Photo Library/Larry
Miller; p. 10, Corbis/Marc Rebutini; p. 11, Science Photo
Library/Jim Reed; p. 12/13, Frank Lane Picture Agency/H
Hoflinger; p.12, Corbis/Tony Arruza ; p. 13, Science Photo
Library/Clem Hagner; p. 14, Corbis/H. David Seawall; p. 15
Corbis/ Bettmann; p. 16/17, Corbis Sygma/Steve Liss; p. 17,
Science Photo Library/Jim Reed; p. 18/19, Corbis/Bettmann; p. 20,
Corbis Sygma/Andrew Hasson; p. 21, Corbis/Reuters; p. 22,
Science Photo Library/Keith Kent; p. 23, Science Photo
Library/Larry Miller; p. 23 right, Corbis Sygma; p. 25, Corbis/Ted
S. Warr; p. 25 right, Corbis/Sunset Boulevard; p. 26, Frank Lane
Picture Agency/David Hoadley; p. 26 left, Science Photo
Library/Jim Reed; p. 27, Science Photo Library/Larry Miller; p. 28,
Corbis/Randy Wells; p. 29, Frank Lane Picture Agency/Jim Reed;
p. 30/31, Corbis/ David Hies; p. 30, Science Photo Library/Jim
Reed; p. 31, Corbis Sygma; p. 32/33, Corbis Sygma/Ted Soqui; p.
32, Corbis Sygma; p. 33, Corbis/Bettmann; p. 34/35, Corbis
Sygma; p. 34, Science Photo Library/Jim Reed; p. 36/37 Corbis
Sygma/Steve Liss; p. 36, Corbis Sygma; p. 37, Corbis Sygma/Salt
Lake Tribune/Galbraith; p. 38, Corbis Sygma/Jim Reed; p. 38 left,
Science Photo Library/Jim Reed; p. 39 Science Photo Library/Jim
Reed; p. 40/41, Frank Lane Picture Agency/Jim Reed; p. 40,
Science Photo Library/ NCAR; p. 41, Science Photo Library/Jim
Reed; p. 42, Frank Lane Picture Agency; p. 42 left, Science Photo
Library/Jim Reed; p. 43, Corbis Sygma/Orlando Sentinel; p. 44,
Science Photo Library/Jim Reed; p. 45, Science Photo
Library/Larry Miller.

Cover photograph reproduced with permission of Getty Images.

Every effort has been made to contact copyright holders of any
material reproduced in this book. Any omissions will be rectified
in subsequent printings if notice is given to the publishers.

Contents

Any words appearing in the text in bold, **like this,** are explained in the Glossary. You can also look out for some of them in the "Stormy Words" box at the bottom of each page.

Twister!

The sunshine fades on a quiet afternoon. The sky grows dark as night. Clouds stretch high into the sky. Lightning flashes and rain pours down. A spinning **funnel** of air drops from the clouds and touches the ground.

Tornadoes are also ▷ called twisters because of the way they turn. The twister at the right is black with the dust it has picked up.

Stormy Words funnel shape like a cone with a wide top that narrows to a tube

Deadly winds

The strongest winds in the world have arrived. They sound like a giant train. The whirling wind rips houses to shreds. **Debris** flies through the air. Suddenly the wind dies and the air quiets. The tornado has passed.

Random killers

Tornadoes, or **twisters**, are the most violent storms on Earth. They can grow to more than half a mile (0.8 kilometers) across. A tornado's winds suck in and destroy anything in its path. Every year in the United States, tornadoes kill about 80 people.

Find out later . . .

. . . *where it is dangerous to hide from a tornado.*

. . . *what kind of clouds might bring a tornado.*

. . . *what a* **waterspout** *is.*

debris   pieces of litter, wrecked houses, cars, and other objects

Tornado Science

Supercells

Huge thunderstorms grow when large blocks of warm air meet cold air. These thunderstorms are called **supercells**. The image below shows a huge thunderstorm in Florida.

Making clouds

A cloud is made up of millions of tiny drops of water or tiny bits of ice. Clouds are formed when warm, wet air moves through colder air.

The air is wet because it contains **water vapor**. The cool air makes the water vapor **condense**. When the vapor condenses it forms tiny water drops.

Thunderclouds

Tornadoes only come out from under huge thunderclouds. Thunderclouds are the biggest clouds of all. They form when warm, moist air

water vapor   water in the form of a gas

rises up in a fast **current** called an **updraft**.

As the air cools, the water vapor condenses to form water drops. These make up huge clouds.

The updraft stops very high above the Earth's surface. When it stops, the cloud spreads out. It then has a shape like a mushroom.

This huge thunderstorm cloud △ has spread out at the top.

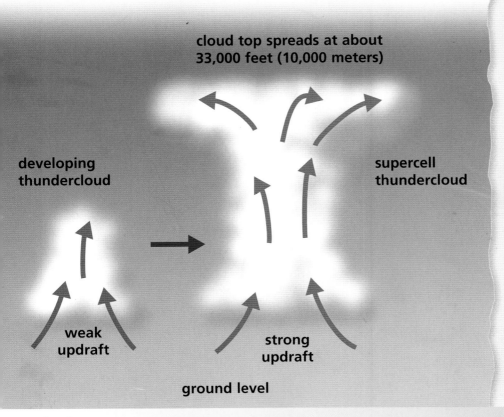

cloud top spreads at about 33,000 feet (10,000 meters)

developing thundercloud

supercell thundercloud

weak updraft

strong updraft

ground level

Cloud shapes

In the drawing at left, warm, moist air rises quickly. As it rises, the air cools. Clouds are formed. The strong updraft creates a bigger thundercloud.

updraft   current of air that flows upward

A spinning storm

Winds can blow in different directions at different levels in the sky. If this happens in a thundercloud, it makes the air inside start to spin. The turning air is pulled into the **updraft**. This makes a column of air rise and spin inside the thunderstorm.

Sometimes the bottom end of the spinning column of air dips below the base of its thundercloud. It sucks up more warm air from under the cloud.

This makes it spin even faster, creating a **vortex**. When the vortex touches the ground, it becomes a tornado.

A wide range of sizes

The average tornado is about 500 feet (150 meters) wide where it touches the ground. Tornadoes can be as small as 165 feet (50 meters) across or as big as 1 mile (1.6 kilometers) across.

Shifting shapes

Some tornadoes look shapeless. Others are very wide. They look like an upside-down bell. Some look like an elephant's trunk. The tornado shown above in Kansas, is shaped like a carrot.

◁ A spinning column of air curves over the road.

vortex   scientific name for a spinning column of air

Inside a tornado

What happens inside a tornado? It is hard to know. It is almost impossible to see inside a tornado.

This is what we know about tornadoes already. The air around the bottom of a tornado is sucked into the **vortex** at great speed. Then it spins upward into the cloud above. The air drags in dust and **debris**. Heavy bits of debris are thrown out sideways as they rise.

Tornado weather

Tornadoes bring rains, often causing **flash floods**. A few hours of heavy rain (see above) caused this flash flood in France.

Inside a tornado ▷ the air swirls around and upward, forming a vortex.

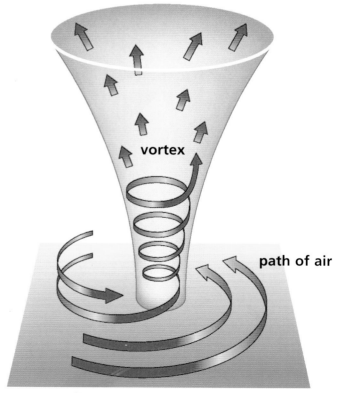

vortex

path of air

flash flood   huge flow of water that happens suddenly because of very heavy rains, or snow melting

View from inside

In the center of a tornado, the air may be clear and move at much lower speeds. We know this because someone has actually seen inside a tornado. In 1943 Roy Hall saw inside a tornado and lived to tell the tale. As the tornado tore his farm apart, Hall looked up into its vortex. He described it as being hollow. The tornado's insides looked like a wobbly pipe that swayed in the wind.

Multiple tornadoes

Some tornadoes break up into smaller, mini tornadoes. The mini tornadoes do just as much harm as the bigger one. Two tornadoes have formed in the picture below.

Waterspouts without water

A waterspout causes ripples on the water below. The swirling wind has not picked up any water. When a waterspout dies out, the water in it drops back into the sea or lake.

Waterspouts

There are several other types of **whirlwind**. In a **waterspout** a column of air spins above water. Strong winds at its base make spray. The waterspout sucks up these drops of water.

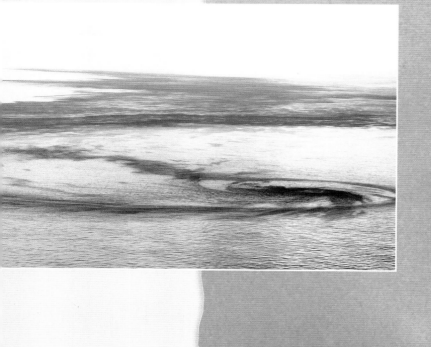

whirlwind   spinning column of air

Dust devils

Another kind of whirlwind is a **dust devil** or land devil. While it looks like a tornado, a dust devil (right) is very different. It starts on the ground instead of in a cloud. Warmed by the sun, the ground heats the air

above it. This hot air rises upward. If the wind swirls around a hillside, it can make the rising air spin. The spinning air picks up dust, straw, and trash from the ground.

◁ A giant waterspout towers over the sea.

dust devil spinning column of air filled with dust, straw, and trash

Measuring tornadoes

How do you measure a tornado? The wind inside would rip the measuring gear from your hands! **Meteorologists** measure a tornado by seeing how much damage it does. The amount of damage can tell us how fast the wind is blowing inside the tornado.

Damage and death

A tornado in Texas caused millions of dollars of damage at the airport shown below.

meteorologist   scientist who studies the weather

The Fujita scale

Theodore Fujita (right) invented
the Fujita Tornado Scale in 1971.
It measures the strength of
tornadoes on a scale of F0 to F5.
F5 tornadoes are the worst. They
cause the most damage.

Mostly harmless

About two thirds of all tornadoes
last only a few minutes and do little
damage. About a third of tornadoes
last twenty minutes or more. Only
2 percent of tornadoes are violent
and continue for more than an hour.

Fujita scale	Wind speed	Type of damage
F0	40–72 miles (64–116 kilometers) per hour	Branches and some windows broken; small trees knocked down
F1	73–112 miles (117–180 kilometers) per hour	Roof tiles ripped off; **mobile homes** moved; large branches broken
F2	113–157 miles (181–253 kilometers) per hour	Whole roofs torn off; mobile homes smashed; some houses lifted off ground; large trees fall
F3	158–206 miles (254–332 kilometers) per hour	Solid walls collapse; trees uprooted; large cars thrown; trains knocked over
F4	207–260 miles (333–418 kilometers) per hour	Houses completely destroyed; cars thrown and smashed; trees fly
F5	more than 261 miles (419 kilometers) per hour	Strong houses thrown around; cars fly through air; trains lifted off ground

mobile home   large trailer that can be put in one place and used as a home

Terrible Tornadoes

Sometimes a single tornado causes a major disaster. Other times a **swarm** of smaller tornadoes does terrible damage. This happened in Oklahoma in 1999. The area looked like a bomb had hit.

Rescue problems

The strong winds in Oklahoma tore down electrical wires and ripped gas pipes apart, causing fires. Rescuers rushed to damaged houses as winds swirled overhead. They faced blackouts, explosions, and fires as they searched for **victims**.

A tornado swarm

On May 3, 1999, swarms of tornadoes touched down in Oklahoma and Kansas. Some of the tornadoes were the worst to ever strike Oklahoma. They were strength F4 on the Fujita scale. Forty-five people were killed.

Disaster in Oklahoma City

One huge **twister** flattened 1,000 homes in Oklahoma City. Thousands of other homes were badly damaged. It ripped sturdy factory buildings to shreds, and threw cars everywhere.

The winds in Oklahoma even tipped over the heavy ▽ truck shown below.

victim   person killed or injured in an accident or bad event

Tornado terror

One tornado hit three states on March 18, 1925. It was the worst tornado on record. The tornado started small, but it grew quickly. It touched down in Ellington, Missouri. Then it headed northeast. After tearing through Annapolis, it sped up. Traveling at 60 miles (100 kilometers) per hour, the tornado flattened Gorham, Illinois. The tornado blew on into Indiana, where it destroyed Griffin and much of Princeton.

A terrible trail

The map below shows the path of the tornado of March 1925. It began in Missouri and ended in Indiana. It destroyed a strip of land 0.75 miles (1.2 kilometers) wide.

A trail of destruction

Finally the tornado died out. It had lasted three and a half hours. In that time, it covered 219 miles (352 kilometers). It wiped out four towns and badly damaged six more.

Nearly 700 people died, including 234 in Murphysboro, Illinois, alone. Thousands more were injured.

Bangladesh
On April 2, 1977, a **swarm** of tornadoes hit Bangladesh. They killed 900 people and 6,000 more were injured.

The tornado of 1925 shredded these homes in Indiana.

Where and When?

Where do tornadoes happen? When are they most common?

British tornadoes

Most tornadoes in the United Kingdom are weak and last only a few minutes. A small tornado ripped out the wall of this British house on the right.

Tornado hot spots

The world's tornado **hot spot** is an area known as Tornado Alley. Between 800 and 1,200 tornadoes hit the United States every year. About 20 measure F4 or F5 on the Fujita scale.

Red dots mark the areas where tornadoes have hit.

▽

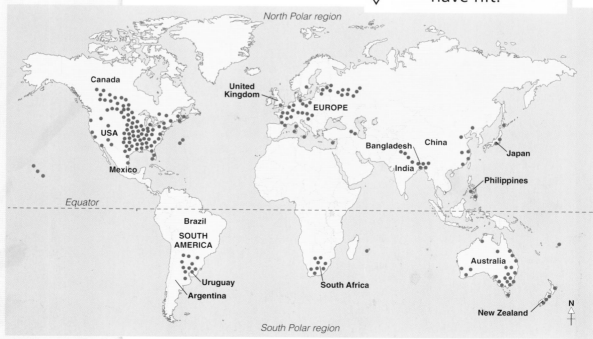

North Polar region

Canada

United Kingdom

EUROPE

USA

Bangladesh   China

Mexico

India   Japan

Philippines

Equator

Brazil

SOUTH AMERICA

Uruguay

Argentina

South Africa

Australia

New Zealand

N

South Polar region

Where fronts meet

Tornadoes happen where moist, warm air meets cold, dry air. The regions where these air masses meet are called **fronts**. Here conditions are perfect to create the violent **supercell** thunderstorms. Tornadoes often come from these supercells.

Australian tornadoes

Tornadoes are quite common in Australia. Most are weak, but some can damage property. Here, a tornado moves toward a boat in the Pacific Ocean between Australia and Tasmania.

front   place where warm air and cold air meet

Tornado times and tracks

Tornadoes strike most often at certain times of year. This is called tornado **season**.

An average tornado lasts less than 10 minutes and travels about 5 miles (8 kilometers). Some die away after a few seconds. Others last for more than an hour. Some hop along. They touch down for a few minutes then lift up again.

Tornado times

Most tornadoes happen in the afternoon, but they can land at night. In this photo, lightning streaks down from a huge, nighttime thunderstorm. It would be hard to see a tornado under the storm at night.

season   period of the year with a specific kind of weather

Tornado tracks

It is hard to tell where a tornado will go. A tornado can speed up, slow down, and swerve from side to side. Some tornadoes travel in huge circles. Some tornadoes can move as fast as a car on a highway. Most go about 35 miles (55 kilometers) per hour.

A tornado ripped apart these homes. It hardly touched other homes only a few hundred feet away. ▽

This tornado could move in any direction. It could touch down on the roads or lift off into the air. ▽

Tornado Alley

One area of the world has more tornadoes than anywhere else. That area stretches across the United States from Texas in the south to North Dakota in the north. It is known as Tornado Alley. On some days, more than twenty tornadoes sweep through Tornado Alley.

Tornado Alley is the home of huge tornadoes. Oklahoma sits right in the middle. More tornadoes hit Oklahoma than any other state.

Alley of death

Tornado Alley is marked in red below. In May 1997 eight tornadoes swept through central Texas. One giant tornado killed more than 30 people in the small town of Jarrell.

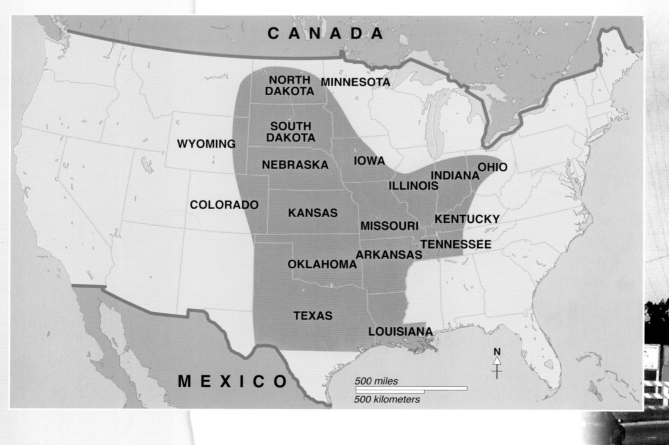

Storms on the plains

Tornado Alley lies on the **plains** between the Gulf of Mexico and the Rocky Mountains. Warm, moist air comes from the Gulf of Mexico. Cold, dry air flows over the Rocky Mountains. They meet and form **supercell** thunderstorms. Supercells can create plenty of tornadoes.

◁ These truck drivers were in great danger from this giant tornado near Jarrell, Texas in 1997.

plains   very flat, wide areas of the countryside

Signs and Warnings

What is it like to be in the path of a huge tornado? How can you protect yourself? What will happen to the buildings? Here is the story of a tornado from start to finish.

Green clouds

Thunderclouds can look slightly green, like those shown at the right. This is often a sign of heavy **hail** (shown below) inside the cloud. Heavy hail shows that a thunderstorm may turn into a tornado.

Gathering clouds

Thunderclouds build up in the sky. The clouds bulge out on top. This shows that the **updrafts** in the cloud are very strong. The storm may be a powerful **supercell**.

More signs

The thunderstorm gets closer. The sky is full of dark clouds. Lumps of clouds hang down from underneath. The tops of the thunderclouds have moved down.

Then the bottom of the thundercloud drops toward the ground. The clouds form into a circle several miles across. They are making a slowly spinning wall. This cloud is called a wall cloud. A wall cloud appears just before many tornadoes touch down.

Clear blue skies

Sunshine does not mean there will be no tornadoes. Sunlight fills the air around the tornado shown below. A tornado sometimes can touch the ground where the sun is shining.

supercell   very violent thunderstorm

Watches and warnings

Weather **forecasters** are always checking for **supercell** thunderstorms. They issue a warning called a tornado watch. This does not mean that someone has seen a tornado. It only means that the weather is right for a tornado to form. People can watch out for one. They should stay tuned to their televisions and radios.

Then, people might hear a tornado warning being **broadcast**. A tornado is likely to touch down very soon or one has already been seen. The tornado warning **siren** is set off.

No shield
Mountains and hills do not protect people from tornadoes. They can sweep over the tops of mountains, as shown here in Montana.

forecaster   person who figures out what the weather will be like in the future

What to do

People should find **shelter** quickly. In areas where there are lots of tornadoes, most schools, offices, and factories have strong tornado shelters. At home people should go into the strongest room in the house. People outside should lie in ditches or under strong bridges over roads.

Safe rooms

A few homes have a room built to stand up to the strongest tornadoes. It is made from steel or concrete. Other people have underground safe rooms like the one shown here.

shelter something that covers or protects

A Tornado Hits

People hide in their **shelters**. Lightning streaks across the dark sky. Loud claps of thunder boom. Heavy rain floods the ground. Giant **hail** stones crash down. The tornado touches down!

The tornado begins to suck up dust as soon as it hits the ground. Warm air from near the ground feeds the tornado. It grows until it is 1,300 feet (400 meters) across.

Moving trees

This tornado in Missouri (below) has uprooted a tree, but left the house behind it alone.

crop   plant that can be grown and sold, usually for food

Tornado damage

Tornadoes do so much damage because of their powerful winds. The winds move, lift, bend, and break all sorts of big and small objects.

The tornado rips **crops** from the field then moves into the woods. Winds pull trees from the ground. Crossing a road, the tornado snaps a line of telephone poles. Drivers leave their cars. The autos are sucked up, hurled out, and destroyed. The tornado even knocks trucks off the road.

Dangerous cars

Cars are not safe places to be during a **twister**. As shown below, a tornado can wrap a car around a tree.

◁ A tornado sweeps through Salt Lake City, Utah. **Debris** flies everywhere.

twister   common name for a tornado

Tornado in town

Now the tornado arrives at the edge of town. **Storm spotters** track its movements. They have radioed ahead to warn people. People hide wherever they feel safe. If they are lucky, the tornado will miss their homes. Scary noises come from close by. Then the tornado arrives. Some people are not lucky, and their houses are destroyed.

Houses

Mobile homes are light, with weak walls and no **basements**. A mini tornado flipped the mobile home shown below.

The tornado has passed. Two people search through what is left of their home.   ▷

storm spotter   person who watches out for tornadoes and warns people

Flattened homes

How can a tornado take apart a house? The fast moving air rushes around and above the house. Winds of 200 miles (320 kilometers) per hour can create a lot of **suction**. They suck the roof right off. This weakens the outside walls of the house. Then the wall facing the wind blows in.

Flying roofs

Tornadoes can even pull the roof off of a factory. A tornado ripped apart the factory shown below.

suction   process of drawing something into a space by removing
           the air from the space

Flying debris

The tornado sucks up objects from streets and destroys houses. The spinning wind throws **debris** toward the outside, like clothes in a washing machine spin cycle. It flings things out of the sides of the **vortex**, for hundreds of feet. These flying objects are a lot more dangerous than the winds.

Everything and the kitchen sink

An F5 tornado can pick up nearly anything in its path. An F5 tornado in Oklahoma grabbed the kitchen sink shown above and wrapped it around a tree.

◁ The twisted metal in this tree is the remains of a road sign that was hurled through the air.

Deadly missiles

A powerful tornado can pick up very big objects. It can lift cars, trucks, and even whole houses. Pieces of houses, fences, street signs, and branches all whizz through the air. They damage anything they hit. Even small objects become deadly at high speeds. Bits of flying glass are a big danger during tornadoes.

A sad scene

The tornado leaves as quickly as it arrived. People come out of their **shelters**. Some are unlucky. Parts of their houses are mixed with broken furniture and smashed televisions and stoves. Their clothes and toys are scattered. Their cars are gone. Though these people have nothing left, they are lucky to be alive.

A narrow strip

The tornado has cut a narrow strip through the town. Inside the strip, everything is destroyed. A few feet away, however, there is no damage. A tornado can wipe out one house but leave the house next door untouched.

Danger comes later

Even after a tornado passes, it is still dangerous. These firefighters are working on the roof. They are checking that the tornado has not loosened any roof tiles that might fall.

Clearing up

Police, **paramedics**, and firefighters arrive. They rush hurt people to the hospital. Then they search for missing people. Shelters with food and beds are set up for homeless people. Sometimes the national guard or army helps rescue people and clean up. The government sometimes gives people money to help rebuild their homes.

Dying away

Many miles away the tornado is finally dying out. It looks like a long, twisting snake. It fades. Then it is gone.

Sad work
Paramedics put an injured person into an ambulance.

◁ There's always a lot to do after a tornado. Here people search through what's left of their homes.

paramedic   person trained in medicine who helps hurt people before taking them to the hospital

Fighting Tornadoes

Tornadoes are very powerful. They kill and hurt people and damage homes and businesses. While we cannot stop them, we can try to find out more about them. Then we will be able to **predict** them and warn people when they are coming.

Weather **researchers** have one big problem. There is very little information about what happens inside tornadoes. It would be crazy to go into a tornado to find out!

Radar on wheels

The truck on the right is called a Doppler on Wheels. **Doppler radar** measures the speed of wind inside clouds. Below a man studies tornadoes inside a Doppler on Wheels.

Future measurement

Another problem for tornado researchers is finding a tornado to research! On average only three occur each day in the entire United States! Researchers have to be in the right place at the right time.

Scientists need information from inside tornadoes. To get it they are developing new machines. New **radar** systems will be able to measure winds inside tornadoes. Scientists are also working on machines called turtles. These small, tough tanks do not need a driver. Scientists direct them while the tanks are inside the **twister**.

Balloons for research

Scientists also use balloons to find out more about tornadoes. The balloon being launched below carries machines to measure what is happening inside the thunderstorm.

radar   machine that uses radio waves to find objects in the distance

Tornado watching

Before a tornado happens, there are often certain kinds of weather. **Meteorologists** know these kinds of weather. They can warn people if tornadoes are likely in their area.

Doppler radar

Below, a **Doppler radar** screen shows thunderstorms. Bright colors show where the strongest winds are.

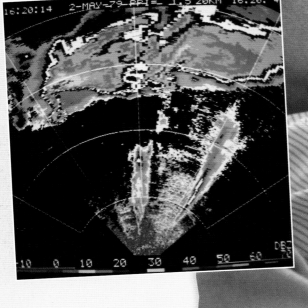

The meteorologists gather information and put it into computers. Computers help figure out what the weather may be like over the next few hours and days. **Forecasters** can then tell people to expect tornadoes.

Meteorologists watch storms ▷ on a computer. The computer uses information from Doppler radar.

Doppler radar   machine that can measure the speed of air moving inside clouds

Storm spotters

Sometimes forecasters see a spinning column of air on their **radar** screens. They warn people by using radio and television that tornadoes may be on the way.

People who live in the area search for tornadoes from their cars. These **storm spotters** report what they see to warning centers. The centers warn people to take **shelter**. Storm spotting is a dangerous job. All storm spotters are trained in safety.

Storm chasers

Storm chasers drive to follow strong thunderstorms in their cars. They hope to see tornadoes. Like the people below, they hope to take pictures or videos of the tornado. Storm chasing is a dangerous hobby.

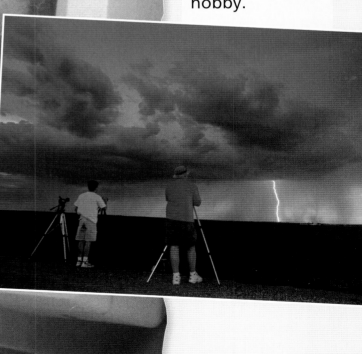

Be ready

There are things you can do to make sure you live through a tornado. You need a place to take **shelter**. You should have a tornado plan like the one on the next page. You must practice your **drill** so you remember what to do if the real thing happens.

You should put together an **emergency** kit. It should include a radio (with extra batteries), a flashlight, a first-aid kit, and a map. You can listen to the radio to find out which way the tornado is going.

Busted bike

Below an F4 tornado wrapped this child's bike around a tree.

When you see a sky like this one, watch out. A tornado ▽ could be on the way.

TORNADO DRILL

- Listen to the radio or watch the television for tornado warnings.
- Go quickly to your tornado shelter, safe room, or **basement**.
- Stay away from windows at all times.
- If a tornado hits, kneel down with your hands over your head.
- Beware of flying **debris**.
- Do not leave your shelter until the all clear signal is given.
- If you are in a car or bus, get out. Lie face down in a ditch with your hands over your head.

Safer and safer

We are getting better at **predicting** tornadoes. Because of this the number of people killed by tornadoes is going down. Today in the United States, about 80 people die each year. In the 1930s, it was 200 a year.

basement   room in the ground under a house

Find Out More

Organizations

The National Weather Service

This is an organization that keeps track of weather conditions around the country. The National Weather Service issues severe weather warnings when necessary. Contact them at the following address:

National Weather Service, National Oceanic and Atmospheric Administration, U.S. Dept. of Commerce, 1325 East West Highway, Silver Spring, MD 20910

Books

Chambers, Catherine. *Tornado: Disasters in Nature*. Chicago: Heinemann Library, 2000.

O'Neill Grace, Catherine. *Forces of Nature: The Awesome Power of Volcanoes, Earthquakes, and Tornados*. Washington, D.C.: National Geographic Childrens, 2004.

Spilsbury, Louise A., and Richard Spilsbury. *Terrifying Tornadoes*. Chicago: Heinemann Library, 2004.

World Wide Web

If you want to find out more about tornadoes, you can search the Internet using keywords such as these:

- tornado +news
- wind +disasters
- tornado +safety

Find your own keywords by using ideas or words from this book. Use the search tips on the next page to help you find the most useful websites.

Search tips

There are billions of pages on the Internet. It can be difficult to find exactly what you are looking for. These tips will help you find useful websites more quickly.

- Decide exactly what you want to find out about first.
- Use simple keywords instead of whole sentences.
- Use two to six keywords in a search, putting the most important words first.
- Be precise—use names of people, places, or things when you can.
- If your keywords are made up of two or more words that go together, put double quote marks around them—for example, "Fujita scale."
- Use the + sign to join keywords together—for example, weather +disaster.

Where to search

Search engine

A search engine looks through millions of website pages. It lists all the sites that match the words in the search box. You will find the best matches are at the top of the list, on the first page.

Search directory

A person instead of a computer has sorted a search directory. You can search by keyword or subject and browse through the different sites. It is like looking through books on a library shelf.

Glossary

basement   room in the ground under a house

broadcast   send information over the radio or television

condense   when a gas turns into a liquid

crop   plant that can be grown and sold, usually for food

current   flow of air or water

debris   pieces of litter, wrecked houses, cars, and other objects

Doppler radar   machine that can measure the speed of air moving inside clouds

drill   way of learning a skill by repeating it

dust devil   spinning column of air filled with dust, straw, and trash

emergency   something serious that happens suddenly

flash flood   huge flow of water that happens suddenly because of very heavy rains or snow melting

forecaster   person who figures out what the weather will be like in the future

front   place where warm air and cold air meet

funnel   shape like a cone with a wide top that narrows to a tube

hail   balls of ice and tightly packed snow

hot spot   place where something happens often

meteorologist   scientist who studies the weather

mobile home   large trailer that can be put in one place and used as a home

paramedic   person trained in medicine who helps hurt people before taking them to hospital

plains   very flat, wide areas of the countryside

predict   say what will happen in the future

radar   machine that uses radio waves to find objects in the distance

researcher   person who collects and studies information about something

season   period of the year with a specific kind of weather

shelter   something that covers or protects

siren   machine that makes a very loud warning noise

storm spotter   person who watches out for tornadoes and warns people

suction   process of drawing something into a space by removing the air from the space

supercell   very violent thunderstorm

swarm   large group of things moving close together

twister   common name for a tornado

updraft   current of air that flows upward

victim   person killed or injured in an accident or bad event

vortex   scientific name for a spinning column of air

water vapor   water in the form of a gas

waterspout   spinning column of air above a sea or lake

whirlwind   spinning column of air

Index